TRADE AND COLLECT
COLLECTABLES

Published by Hartley Publications Ltd.
P.O. Box 100, Devizes, Wiltshire, SN10 4TE

Typeset, make-up and printing by
Wentrow Media,
49 Lancaster Road, Bowerhill Trading Estate,
Melksham, Wiltshire, SN12 6SS

Contents

Introduction

Welcome to Trade And Collect Collectables.

This book has been written as a comprehensive introduction to the world of collecting. As well as being a fully-illustrated, full-colour price guide, the book is also filled with useful information and advice.

The hobby of collecting is getting more and more popular, with extensive television coverage; and we don't believe there is any better time to start your own collection than right now.

For ease of use, the book has been divided into four distinct sections:

1. A general introduction to collecting, containing plenty of helpful advice for novices and experts alike.

2. A wonderfully illustrated guide, covering a wide range of items that have been sold at auction. The prices realised are given, so as well as being interesting, the listing can also give you a useful insight into market trends. You may even find a few things here that you have in your own collection.

3. Tables and charts of reference material on specific subjects that will be invaluable in your quest for collectable items.

4. A glossary of collecting terms.

Whatever you decide to collect, we hope this little book will become a vital part of your collecting experience.

Best of luck with your treasure hunting.

Investing in Collectables Items

Many collectors collect for fun – there is a subject they are interested in, and they collect relating to that subject. However, there are many other collectors who look on collecting as a business. As with any business, buying low and selling high is the name of the game; and it is important to acquire stock that has a strong chance of selling for profit.

While there is no guarantee that a particular collectable item represents an investment potential, there is little doubt that many items do. The following guidelines should assist in procuring good quality items.

- Look for items that are not likely to have been deemed collectable in the first place, or items that are rare and unusual. Scarcity drives up the value, so uncommon items will often (although not always) represent a better investment.

- Concentrate on items that are small. Not only does this make items easier to store, but it also makes them easier to post should you decide to sell them to someone who isn't able to collect the item in person.

- Look for unusual items in current day-to-day use NOW and store them away safely.

- Concentrate on a particular subject. If you focus your collecting, it will stop your collection from becoming too large and you will start to become an expert. If you know a lot about your subject, then you will know the best times to sell, the best places to sell, and the right prices to be asking for.

- While you may build your collection on the basis that an item of any condition will do, it is recommended you collect only the best quality possible to improve investment potential.

- Log every item in your collection and take photographs. This will function as a stock list as well as being useful for insurance purposes. Make sure you store the stock list and photographs in a different location to where you store the actual items.

- Do your homework. Do not buy items without establishing if you are buying at a good price. Also, make sure you know how to recognise fake and reproduction items.

Storing Collectable Items

- Always package your items individually, with a note specifying the date the item was purchased and how much you paid. Notes on the item's history may also prove useful.

- For paper items, include a backing board, slightly larger than the item itself. Do NOT fold the items.

- Flat items, such as vinyl records, should be stored upright to avoid bowing.

- Never store items in a place where there may be vermin. For safety's sake, your items should be stored inside containers.

- Avoid using sticky tape to seal plastic bags, as there is a risk the tape may get stuck to an item and ruin it. Try to use bags with a plastic interlocking seal strip instead.

- Do not wrap silver items in newspapers or put rubber bands around items such as spoons. This leaves marks that are difficult to remove.

- Never wrap decks of cards or postcards with rubber bands, as this can irreparably damage the cardstock.

- Rare books should be stored rather than read. Opening the pages of old books can cause damage.

- Do not stack boxes on top of other boxes unless absolutely necessary. If you have to stack some boxes, make sure you stack bigger boxes ON TOP OF smaller boxes, as this will prevent the weight of the smaller boxes causing the lids of bigger boxes to be crushed or bowed.

- Store all items in a cool dark place. A loft may experience extremes of temperature so may not be ideal.

- Do not clean old items before storing them, unless you are sure that cleaning the items will not cause any harm.

Buying at Car Boot Sales

- Arrive early to catch the real treasures.

- Take a rucksack to carry what you buy.

- Make sure you have plenty of small change.

- Take a supply of plastic bags and some A4 plastic or card wallets for protecting your purchases.

- Watch out for pickpockets.

- The first stall you visit should be the latest one to set up.

- Dress like a pauper, so it's easier to haggle.

- Be careful when buying electrical items, they may not be safe to use. They may not work at all.

- ALWAYS HAGGLE.

- Be prepared to get down on your hands and knees to sift through boxes of oddments. Some great little treasures can be found at the bottom of a box of "junk".

- Never show excitement. A deadpan expression is required with every offer.

- Don't take your dog. Many boot sales now ban them.

- If it is a hot day, remember to take some sun cream. Conversely, if it is a cold day, wrap up warm.

- Take your own food and a flask of coffee, so you don't have to waste time queuing at the refreshment stands.

- Don't push and shove when looking at a stall. Boot sales are supposed to be friendly affairs.

- Tender the exact sum negotiated.

- Don't try to outbid someone else on an item he or she has already picked up. It's commonly accepted that once you hold an item in your hand, it's your first option.

- Don't be aggressive when you haggle.

- Don't tell a seller that his or her items are rubbish.

- Don't interfere with someone else's sale. Let the buyer and seller negotiate the arrangement themselves.

Selling at Car Boot Sales

- Don't take items that can be easily damaged.

- Be positive. If asked for a "best price", don't respond in a quizzical tone of voice, as if to say "Is that all right?"

- Do not put items aside for potential purchasers for any reason, unless you take a non-refundable deposit first.

- Take plenty of empty plastic bags and newspaper to wrap items.

- Don't keep your money anywhere that requires you to turn your back on your stall.

- Placing an item in a clear plastic wallet can give it a feeling of being valuable, and allows you to attach a price sticker without causing damage.

- Try placing price tags underneath items, forcing potential buyers to pick up the items and turn them over. This gives you a clear indication of their interest. (Please note: this suggestion is not recommended for breakable items.)

- If the weather looks like it will be unpredictable, take a gazebo with you. These can be purchased quite cheaply from household stores, and can be a real lifesaver if you get caught in a downpour.

- When using a fold-up table, cover it with a white or cream sheet. This will help bring out the colour in your sale items, and will generally make the stall look more attractive. Your items may look even more valuable.

What is it Worth?

A typical example of an item that can be found at a Collectors' Fair is a 1964 Butlin's (Minehead) badge, and many people will be aware of the value of such an item (approximately £5 - £7). Hence, when you offer a mere £2, the seller will politely advise you of the situation.

What the seller really needs to do is bring hundreds of Butlin's badge collectors together and auction his badge. If he can do this, he is likely to achieve a top market value. However, to bring enough people together can be costly, and this (hidden) cost eventually has to be passed on to the buyer.

If you remove this costly element of finding the right buyer (for example, selling the badge among many other items on a car boot stall) the actual cost of the sale becomes much less and therefore the selling price should be below the expected top retail value.

Many sellers quote "book price" to justify a high price, but car boot sales are not the ideal place to sell a specialised item, if top retail value is sought.

Now, once you have politely explained the theory to the seller you can proceed to buy at below the "true value" and, once you have acquired the item, set about your task of making a profit in a wider marketplace.

Social History

A tiny scrap of paper, often perceived as rubbish, can actually have meaning and significance in terms of social history. An example would be an old sweet wrapper.

It is not desirable to keep all sweet wrappers or every scrap of paper, but selective saving (particularly of items in excellent condition) can result in collectable items for the future.

In the example of a sweet wrapper, this becomes so much more desirable when the product has long ceased production; even more so if the manufacturer has ceased trading completely.

Did the manufacturer employ large numbers of people? Did the area rely heavily on that company for livelihoods and social activities? Some people may have devoted their entire lives to that one company. Summer holidays may even have been influenced by the company, with social club visits to the seaside, etc.

Social history is generally fascinating, and collectors are helping to preserve it for generations to come. Car boot sales are playing a role, although many people are totally unaware.

On a more financial note, documenting the historical background to a collectable item will nearly always add value to it.

Provenance

Provenance concerns evidence of the origin and history of ownership of a particular item.

Provenance can be proved in all manner of ways, from scientific methods to something as simple as a shop receipt or deed of ownership, and may considerably increase the value of your treasures. For example, a library stamp in a book could link the book to a person or place of historical importance, causing the investment potential of the book to increase.

Obviously, such provenance can be faked, and the collector should be wary of this. The more evidence of provenance there is, the more likely the item is to be genuine, and the more interesting the item will be.

Proving provenance is not always easy, but you should be conscious of it. For example, if you get the chance to acquire a famous person's autograph:

1.   Take a photograph of the autograph being written, using a
        camera that has a time and date stamp.

2.   Get the autograph on something dated (like a concert
        programme).

This not only helps to prove the autograph is genuine, but gives the autograph a place in history.

The Guide to Collectables

Collecticus is a monthly magazine featuring all manner of collectable items. Every item featured in the magazine subsequently goes up for sale at auction with a start price of just 1p. Subscribers can bid on the items by post or by using the Collecticus website.

On the following pages, we have featured a wide range of items that were sold through the Collecticus auction.

For each item we have included a brief description, a year of manufacture or issue, the condition (see below), the date when sold, and the price the item realised in the auction.

Dates in brackets are estimated.

Letters in brackets indicate the condition of the item:

Poor = p
Fair = f
Good = g
Very Good = vg
Excellent = ex
Mint = mnt

Conditions are sometimes combined. For example (p-f).

▲ AA grille badge. 1945. (f-g).
Sold 24 May 2007: £18.70

AA memorabilia in general is very desirable at the moment, but grille badges are arguably the most popular items (see page 67).

The first AA badge was issued in March 1906, nine months after the initial formation of the Automobile Association. In 1945, the AA badge was completely redesigned, incorporating a permanent yellow backing plate. The square grille badge was first introduced in 1967.

Collectors of AA memorabilia are also very interested in keys, ashtrays, handbooks, models and staff pin badges.

▲ Dinky motorcycle patrol. 1959-1962.
(g). Sold 5 February 2007: £23.60

▲ AA grille badge. (1975). (g).
Sold 26 July 2007: £4.00

Action Man

◄ Action Man sailor. 1970. (vg). Sold 14 August 2006: £150.10

► Action Man adventurer (reproduction). 2006. (mnt). Sold 26 February 2008: £16.00

CONTAINING REAL CREAM

CANADA
BAR 6 D.

▲ Canada Bar tin sign. (1960). 640 x 122mm. (g).
Sold 24 April 2006: £21.10

▲ Newcastle Brown Ale tin sign. (1955).
610 x 388mm. (g).
Sold 9 October 2006: £27.50

▲ Platignum pens tin sign. (1965). 320
x 245mm (vg).
Sold 23 May 2006: £15.10

MICHELIN TYRES

▲ Michelin Tyres tin sign. (1955). 470 x 32mm. (f).
Sold 3 January 2008: £12.00

Aeronautica is the term for items relating to airlines and aviation. This is a superb collecting area to specialise in, as there are plenty of small items available, meaning they are easy to store. Many items are available at affordable prices.

With so much material available, the clever collector has the luxury of picking and choosing. One tip is to concentrate on airlines that no longer exist. For example, anything relating to BOAC is desirable. If you concentrate on one particular airline, such as BOAC, you will be kept busy and you can always upgrade your collection with better condition examples and trade your duplicates.

Perhaps the most desirable aeronautica of the moment is anything relating to Concorde, but with many airlines going out of business or changing their names, it pays to collect just about anything that is on offer at a very low price. Of course, you should always save your own airline tickets, keeping them in mint condition.

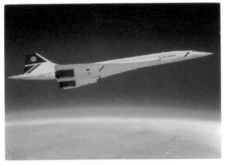

▲ British Airways Concorde postcard. (1985). (vg). Sold 24 May 2007: £3.70

▲ Concorde pencil sharpener. (1980). (vg). Sold 23 August 2007: £11.00

▲ BOAC beer mat. (1960). (g). Sold 26 July 2007: £4.10

▲ Aircraft spotter cards. (1943). (g). Sold 23 August 2007: £20.10

▲ The Sweeney. 1976. (vg). Sold 6 May 2008: £6.40

▲ Batman with Robin the Boy Wonder. 1966. (vg). Sold 8 April 2008: £15.10

▲ Voyage to the Bottom of the Sea. 1968. (vg). Sold 29 september 2008: £14.60

▲ Gunsmoke. 1964 (vg). Sold 29 september 2008: £10.10

▲ Jim Henson's Muppet Show Annual. 1979. (vg). Sold 29 August 2006: £6.10

▲ Roy of the Rovers. 1973. (vg). Sold 25 March 2008: £8.10

▲ Joanna Lumley autographed photo. (ex). Sold 11 March 2008: £15.50

▲ Kylie Minogue autographed photo. (mnt). Sold 11 September 2006: £36.50

▲ Kate Beckinsale autographed photo. (vg). Sold 3 January 2008: £20.10

▲ The Highway Code. 1959. (g). Sold 6 May 2008: £6.00

▲ Ford Zephyr ashtray. (1970). (g). Sold 25 March 2008: £8.10

▲ Ford Prefect Instruction book. 1959. (f-g). Sold 17 July 2008: £10.10

Babycham

▲ Giant Babycham beer mat. (1960). (g). Sold 14 August 2006: £7.60

▲ Babycham plastic deer. (1965). (vg). Sold 26 July 2007: £22.90

▲ Babycham tea towel. (1965). (vg). Sold 14 August 2006: £35.30

▲ Babycham glass. (1970). (g). Sold 5 February 2008: £15.10

Badges

▲ Post Office. (1965). (vg). Sold 22 August 2005: £6.00

▲ Silver dog head . (1980). (g). Sold 19 October 2005: £15.20

▲ Spratts. (1975). (ex). Sold 8 April 2008: £10.10

▲ Asterix . 1978. (g). Sold 21 June 2007: £1.20

▲ George VI Coronation . 1937. (f). Sold 19 October 2005: £12.10

▲ House Captain . (1985). (ex). Sold 20 March 2006: £5.00

▲ Elvis Costello . (1975). (vg). Sold 27 September 2007: £1.30

▲ Gas . (1975). (g). Sold 15 April 2008: £1.10

Ballroom

▲ Ballroom Dancing book. 1979. (g). Sold 27 September 2007: £3.00

▲ Modern Ballroom Dancing book. 1939. (f). Sold 27 September 2007: £5.00

▲ Victor Silvester autographed card. (1940). (vg). Sold 27 September 2007: £50.20

Banknotes

▲ "White fiver". 1956. (ex). Sold 26 July 2007: £135.90

We would recommend you do not begin seriously investing in banknotes unless you first know what you are doing.

Store your banknotes flat and never fold them. Take particular care with the corners. Values depend on rarity and condition. A scruffy note is worth a fraction of a mint/excellent example, and you should always keep an eye open for fakes.

▲ Tiny Chihuahua Beanie Baby. 1998. (ex). Sold 20 February 2006: £8.10

▲ Specs Beanie Kids Beanie Baby. 2001. (ex). Sold 19 December 2005: £10.00

▲ Amber Beanie Baby. 1999. (vg). Sold 26 July 2007: £8.00

Beanie Babies have fallen out of favour with collectors in recent years, and it is now possible to pick up examples for just a few pounds that might once have set you back £50 or more. This is not to say that there is no market for Beanie Babies, it just means you need to carefully research your purchases before you buy or you might end up out of pocket. Remember that there are still some Beanies that sell for hundreds of pounds - the trick is to find out which ones.

▲ The Beatles – All My Loving vinyl EP. 1964. (g). Sold 9 May 2006: £20.00

▲ Liverpool Echo: John Lennon Shot Dead. 1980. (g). Sold 21 November 2005: £25.00

▲ Meet The Beatles – Star Special. 1963. (vg). Sold 5 February 2008: £14.20

▲ Lennon commemorative cover. 1980. (vg). Sold 6 November 2006: £15.10

◀ Beatles ear rings. (1975). (vg). Sold 8 January 2007: £10.00

Breweriana

▲ Comic postcard. 1907. (f-g). Sold 1 April 2008: £6.10

▲ Gordon's Gin matchbook. (1980). (f). Sold 8 January 2007: £5.50

▲ Johnny Walker whisky jug. (1975). (vg). Sold 26 April 2007: £30.90

Butlin's

All Butlin's memorabilia is collectable, and is likely to increase in value. Badges are particularly popular, and make solid investments.

As always, look out for early examples in very good condition or better, and be sure you are buying genuine items (not reproductions).

▲ Bognor Regis resin coated badge. 2004. (ex). Sold 15 April 2008: £15.10

▲ Pwllheli enamel badge. 1957. (g). Sold 15 April 2008: £14.10

▲ Ayr enamel badge. 1954. (g-vg). Sold 8 April 2008: £18.00

▲ Bognor Regis enamel badge. 1962. (vg). Sold 25 March 2008: £10.20

▲ Clacton enamel badge. 1951. (g). Sold 18 March 2008: £20.10

Cigarette Cards

▲ Our King and Queen. 1937. WD&HO Wills. (vg). Sold 20 May 2008: £40.00

▲ Speed. 1938. WD&HO Wills. (vg). Sold 22 April 2008: £25.00

▲ The Doncella Golden Age of Sail. 1980. John Player. (ex). Sold 12 February 2008: £16.00

Cigarette Packets

▲ Flag. (1920). (g-vg). Sold 18 March 2008: £16.50

▲ Park Drive. (1945). (g). Sold 6 May 2008: £5.10

▲ Tenner. (1935). (f). Sold 6 May 2008: £10.10

Coca-Cola

Coca-Cola memorabilia is a hot collecting area at the moment. Old tin signs, metal serving trays, and unopened bottles are in high demand. Christmas-themed items are also very popular, thanks to Coca-Cola's long-term association with the image of Father Christmas.

▲ Unopened bottle. 2003. (ex). Sold 3 January 2008: £5.00

▲ Coca-Cola mechanical money bank. 1995. (vg). Sold 11 March 2008: £31.60

▲ The Best of Eagle. 1988. (g-vg). Sold 24 May 2007: £3.00

▲ Playtime. 1919. (f). Sold 23 August 2007: £6.00

▲ Battle Action. 1978. (g-vg). Sold 5 February 2008: £2.50

▲ Hotspur. 1949. (g). Sold 18 March 2008: £11.10

▲ Buzz comic (issue one with free gift). 1973. (vg). Sold 22 August 2005: £32.70

▲ Cor!! 1974. (g). Sold 25 October 2007: £1.00

▲ Knockout. 1971. (g). Sold 11 March 2008: £3.10

▲ The Beano. 1964. (g). Sold 18 March 2008: £12.40

▲ The Hotspur. 1968. (g-vg). Sold 21 June 2007: £6.10

▲ The Beano. 1954. (f). Sold 3 January 2008: £10.10

▲ Strange Tales. 1965. (f-g). Sold 11 March 2008: £5.60

▲ Valiant. 1969. (g). Sold 29 April 2008: £4.10

▲ The Hornet. 1969. (g). Sold 26 July 2007: £6.10

▲ Playtime. 1920. (g). Sold 5 February 2008: £10.00

▲ Buster. 1969. (g). Sold 18 March 2008: £9.10

▲ Whoopee! 1976. (g). Sold 29 April 2008: £3.00

▲ Two boys with chick puzzle. (1945). (g). Sold 10 June 2008: £7.30

▲ R Journet "Speech Day" puzzle. (1945). (g). Sold 26 February 2008: £11.30

▲ Juggling puzzle. (1935). (f). Sold 26 February 2008: £6.70

▲ R Journet "The Discuss" puzzle. (1950). (vg). Sold 19 February 2008: £12.60

▲ R Journet "Golden Rod" puzzle. (1950). (g). Sold 4 March 2008: £6.90

▲ R Journet "Geometrical" puzzle. (1950). (g-vg). Sold 27 September 2007: £8.00

Disneyana

▲ Mickey Mouse yo-yo. (1990). (vg). Sold 22 April 2008: £4.30

▲ Goofy Annual. 1975. (vg). Sold 1 April 2008: £5.00

▲ Commonwealth of Dominica First Day Cover. 1984. (vg-ex). Sold 4 March 2008: £6.20

Dolls

▲ Pedigree vinyl doll. (1965). (ex). Sold 21 June 2007: £25.00

▲ Black Rosebud doll. (1952). (vg). Sold 21 June 2007: £25.00

▲ German bisque head doll. (1910). (ex). Sold 21 June 2007: £90.00

Elvis

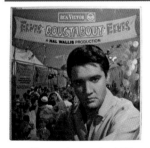

▲ Roustabout vinyl LP. (1964) (g-vg). Sold 26 February 2008: £20.00

▲ Graceland pin badge. (1990). Boxed. (g-vg). Sold 3 July 2006: £18.00

▲ Elvis Monthly 236. 1979. (vg). Sold 1 September 2008: £6.30

Ephemera

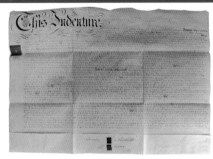

▲ Indenture certificate. 1860. (f). Sold 22 April 2008: £10.10

Ephemera generally refers to anything that was designed to be used and then thrown away, and as such it covers such a diverse range of items as railway tickets, postage stamps, theatre tickets and programmes, letters, telegrams, birthday cards, advertising, notices, and newspapers. Although ephemera items are normally paper, they can actually be made from any material.

▲ Southampton vs Manchester City. 1972. (g). Sold 20 May 2008: £6.50

▲ Chelsea v Manchester United FA Cup. 2007 final. (ex). Sold 23 August 2007: £16.10

▲ Newcastle United vs Blackpool. 1960. (g). Sold 22 April 2008: £7.50

Games

A lot of game collectors actually like to play with their collection, so games should always be complete and playable. You should also pay particular attention to the box, which is often just as important as what's inside. The cover image should be bright, and the corners should be free from tears and scruffs.

▲ Conquest. (1976). (g). Sold 3 January 2008: £4.10

▲ Evening Party Games. (1945). (g). Sold 5 February 2008: £6.50

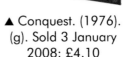

▲ Ludo. (1960). (f). Sold 26 April 2007: £9.60

▲ Impertinent Questions. (1945). (g).Sold 5 February 2008: £7.60

▲ Tell Me. (1970). (vg).Sold 3 January 2008: £6.20

Gollies

▲ Golly figurine. (1960). (vg). Sold 18 March 2008: £12.10

▲ Golden Shred enamel golly badge. (1965). (g). Sold 29 April 2008: £35.10

▲ Golly paper token. (1965). (g). Sold 21 June 2007: £1.10

Gramophone Needles

▲ Columbia. (1940). (g). Sold 6 May 2008: £7.60

▲ Eddison Bell. (1930). (g). Sold 6 May 2008: £16.60

▲ His Master's Voice. (1930). (g). Sold 6 May 2008: £12.10

Guinness

▲ Guinness glass goblet. 2000. (ex). Sold 13 May 2008: £30.00

▲ Guinness bottle tops. (1970). (vg). Sold 19 February 2008: £1.00

Guinness now has an iconic status, meaning any item branded with the Guinness logo (especially unusual items) will prove popular with collectors. Look out for good examples where the famous harp is nice and clear.

Old advertisements featuring the artwork of John Gilroy are also a big draw for collectors.

Magazines

▲ Small Trader and Wholesaler. 1961. (g). Sold 22 April 2008: £2.30

▲ Look-In. 1981. (vg). Sold 25 March 2008: £5.60

▲ Popswop. 1974. (vg). Sold 4 March 2008: £4.00

▲ Understanding Science. 1962. (g). Sold 15 April 2008: £1.00

▲ The Boy's Own Paper. 1892. (g). Sold 22 November 2007: £4.20

▲ Picture Show. 1949. (g). Sold 22 November 2007: £2.10

▲ Look-In. 1977. (g). Sold 18 March 2008: £10.00

▲ Look-In. 1980. (vg). Sold 4 March 2008: £3.60

▲ Punch. 1911. (f-g). Sold 19 February 2008: £5.10

Matchbooks

▲ Maison Prunier. (1950). (g). Sold 5 February 2008: £2.10

▲ Playboy Club (London). (1960). (g). Sold 5 February 2008: £3.50

A collection of match-books can be built up relatively quickly, and for little expense. To help you along, ask all of your friends and relatives to pick up matchbooks whenever they are away (at a hotel, golf course, holiday resort). Don't worry if you end up with "doubles", you can always sell or trade them.

▲ Complete set of Noddy books. 1960s. (g).
Sold 23 May 2005: £90.10

Observer's Books

▲ Garden Flowers.
1980. (vg). Sold 22 August
2005: £6.60

Observer's Books all have print codes that can be used to determine when the book was printed. These codes can be found in the front or the back of the book and appear as two numbers separated by a full stop (for example, 641.1261 or 738.662). The number before the full stop is the printer's code, the number after the full stop represents the month and year of printing (for example, 641.1261 means printer's code 641, produced in December 1961; 738.662 means printer's code 738, produced in June 1962).

▲ Birds. 1956. (g). Sold 18
January 2006: £6.10

▲ Aircraft. 1979. (vg). Sold 9
October 2006: £5.10

▲ Heraldry. 1968. (vg). Sold
6 November 2006: £5.30

Pelham Puppets

Bob Pelham launched his famous Pelham Puppets in 1947 after serving in the 2nd World War. Bob Pelham died in 1980 and his widow carried on the business until 1986. After that, Pelham Puppets changed hands four times before going into receivership in 1992.

It is quite often the case that the boxes for dolls and other toys were discarded by children, who saw no further use for them. However, this does not apply to Pelham Puppets. Because the puppets had strings that could easily become tangled, it was common for children to keep returning the puppets to their rightful boxes after playtime to keep them tidy. This is good news for all the collectors out there, who benefit from an increased chance of finding Pelham Puppets that are still in the original packaging, although this does mean a boxed Pelham is not significant a find as same items.

▲ Charlie Brown. 1966. Unboxed. (g). Sold 13 May 2008: £10.70

▲ Witch. (1970). Boxed. (f). Sold 18 December 2006: £30.00

▲ Mitzi. (1970). Boxed. (g). Sold 27 September 2007: £40.10

▲ Pluto. (1965). Boxed. (vg). Sold 8 April 2008: £37.60

Playing Cards

▲ Batman. 1989. (g).
Sold 23 May 2005:
£4.10

▲ HMS Renown. (1954).
(g). Sold 19 February
2007: £9.50

▲ James Bond. 2001.
(g). Sold 20 May 2008:
£7.50

Railwayana

▲ British Rail cap and badge. (1980).
(g). Sold 22 August 2005: £15.00

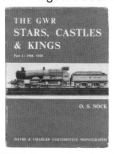

▲ The GWR Stars, Castles & Kings.
1967. (g). Sold 11 March 2008: £8.10

▲ British Railways Rule Book. 1950. (g).
Sold 1 April 2008: £10.50

▲ New Street Station postcard. (1905).
(g). Sold 1 April 2008: £20.00

▲ GWR enamel pin badge. 1985. (g).
Sold 25 September 2006: £5.10

▲ Torbay Express GWR King George V
postcard. (1930). (g). Sold 18 February
2008: £6.10

▲ Pat Boone – Four by Pat. 1957. (f). Sold 20 March 2006: £5.30

▲ Waltzing Through the Roaring 20s. (1955). (g). Sold 22 March 2007: £2.30

▲ Chubby Checker's Dancin' Party. 1962. (g). Sold 21 June 2007: £10.00

▲ Roy Orbison – In Dreams. 1963. (f). Sold 23 May 2006: £6.00

▲ Beach Boys – Surfin' USA. 1963. (vg). Sold 21 June 2007: £14.00

▲ The Shadows to the Fore. 1961. (vg). Sold 21 June 2007: £12.10

▲ Nat King Cole and George Shearing. 1962. (vg). Sold 3 July 2006: £5.00

▲ Paul Robeson – Sanders of the River. 1956. (g). Sold 21 June 2007: £6.60

▲ The Byrds – Eight Miles High. 1967. (g). Sold 21 June 2007: £11.10

Royalty

▲ Oxo Commemorative tin. 1953. (g). Sold 20 February 2006: £10.70

▲ Coronation souvenir programme. 1953. (g). Sold 23 May 2006: £7.00

▲ Benbros Queen Elizabeth II model. (1957). (ex). Sold 21 April 2005: £50.10

Sheet Music

▲ Sitting in the Back Seat. 1959. (vg). Sold 26 February 2008: £9.00

▲ Atmosphere. 1984. (f). Sold 13 May 2008: £3.10

▲ Funny How Love Can Be. 1965. (g). Sold 5 February 2008: £10.50

Snoopy

▲ Snoopy money box. (1975). (g). Sold 23 August 2007: £20.10

▲ Snoopy McDonald's toy. 1999. (g). Sold 9 October 2006: £3.60

▲ Snoopy and the Red Baron View-Master reel. 1969. (vg). Sold 4 March 2008: £5.50

Star Wars

▲ Darth Vader bubble bath. 1977. (g). Sold 18 January 2006: £9.30

▲ Kenner Obi-Wan Kenobi action figure. 1977. (vg). Sold 27 September 2007: £8.10

▲ Anthony Daniels (C-3PO) autographed cartoon. (vg). Sold 27 September 2007: £11.10

The collecting of expired vehicle tax discs is known as 'velology'. People have been collecting for years but it's only just beginning to be treated seriously. Most dealers in automobilia are aware that tax discs, particularly old ones, have value. Like most collectibles, condition is very important and here lies a problem. Motorists place their new tax discs in windscreens and they often fade and can easily be damaged.

▲ June 1933 quarterly tax disc. (g). Sold 25 October 2007: £200.10

Tax discs became a legal requirement from 1 January 1921 and the first expiry date was the end of March that year.

Telephones

◄ Mickey Mouse telephone. (2000). (vg). Sold 21 July 2005: £27.20

◄ Ring dial telephone. 1940. (g). Sold 18 December 2006: £20.10

◄ Chameleon telephone. (2000). (vg). Sold 21 June 2007: £50.10

◄ Tigger telephone. (2000). (g). Sold 25 October 2007: £18.00

◄ Trimphone. (1970). (vg). Sold 12 February 2008: £25.00

▲ National Dried Milk tin. (1950). (g). Sold 2 February 2008: £10.70

▲ Victory V Lozenges tin. (1975). (vg). Sold 5 February 2007: £8.70

▲ Hacks Menthold and Eucalyptus tin. (1900). (f). Sold 5 February 2007: £15.70

▲ Chinese Design Huntley & Palmers tin. (1925). (g-vg). Sold 2 February 2008: £5.60

▲ Casket design Huntley & Palmers tin. 1913. (f-g). Sold 2 February 2008: £25.00

▲ Quality Street tin. 1959. (g). Sold 2 February 2008: £4.20

▲ Princess Mary gift tin. No contents.1914. (vg). Sold 18 January 2006: £30.50

Tobacciana is the term used for items relating to tobacco. It's a huge subject with hundreds of different companies involved, many of which are no longer in existence. You could consider collecting items relating to a particular brand.

▲ Manikin cigars tin. (1975). (vg). Sold 11 March 2008: £4.60

▲ Wooden cigarette case. (1930). (g). Sold 20 February 2006: £8.20

▲ Marlboro ashtray. (1990). (vg). Sold 15 April 2008: £10.00

▲ Player's Navy Cut gift box. (1925). (f-g). Sold 19 December 2005: £10.10

▲ Player's Navy Cut Queen Elizabeth coronation tin. 1953. (vg). Sold 23 August 2007: £20.10

▲ Rothmans letter opener. (1975). (ex). Sold 25 September 2006: £8.00

◄ Senior Service swizzle stick. (1965). (vg). Sold 19 February 2008: £5.00

◄ Kensitas tin sign. (1950). 512 x 170mm. (vg). Sold 21 June 2007: £40.10

Toffee Hammers

▲ McCowans. (2000). (g).
Sold 12 February 2008: £3.00

▲ Sharps. (1960). (g).
Sold 12 February 2008: £3.10

Toys

▲ Meccano instruction booklet. (1950).
(f). Sold 26 February 2008: £6.10

▲ Frankonia tinplate tank. (1965). (g).
Sold 22 June 2005: £20.00

▲ Tinplate Royal Navy staff car. (1950).
(g). Sold 4 March 2008: £12.00

◀ Tinplate spinning
top. (1950). (vg).
Sold 25 October
2007: £21.00

▲ Jirojex tinplate jet plane. (1940). (f).
Sold 23 May 2006: £22.30

◀ Cup Final bagatelle.
(1960). (vg). Sold 26
July 2007: £15.00

◀ Wild West Spin Dart game.
(1950). (vg). Sold 23 August
2007: £24.40

▲ Set of 50 Cadet Stingray sweet cards. 1965. (vg).
Sold 21 June 2007: £28.20

▲ Set of 80 A&BC Flags cards. 1960. (g).
Sold 21 June 2007: £75.20

World War I

◄ "To My Dear Wife" postcard. 1918. (f). Sold 29 April 2008: £10.00

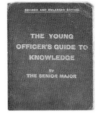

◄ Young Officer's Guide to Knowledge. 1915. (f). Sold 21 February 2005; £7.70

◄ Comic postcard. 1915. (g). Sold 26 April 2007: £11.00

◄ Old Contemptibles Association lapel badge. (1914). (vg). Sold 22 August 2005: £22.60

▲ WWII 50th Anniversary Commemorative Cover. 1989. (vg). Sold 12 February 2008: £10.80

▲ Used envelope "on active service" from South India. 1941. (g). Sold 20 March 2006: £2.10

▲ National Service Act Certificate of Registration. 1939. (g). Sold 8 April 2008: £25.10

▲ 8th Army Desert Rats cloth patch. (1944). (g). Sold 27 September 2007: £15.00

◄ Air Raid Precaution whistle. (1940). (g). Sold 20 March 2006: £15.50

◄ National Identity Card. 1940. (g). Sold 23 May 2005: £7.00

◄ Air Raid Precaution badge. (1940). (g). Sold 23 August 2007: £11.00

◄ Royal Observer Corps Badge. (1941). (vg). Sold 18 January 2006: £12.70

◄ Air Raid Precaution lamp. (1940). (ex). Sold 21 April 2005: £35.90

◄ AFV Recognition information. 1942. (f-g). Sold 26 April 2007: £7.00

Roman Numerals

1	I
2	II
3	III
4	IV
5	V
6	VI
7	VII
8	VIII
9	IX
10	X
11	XI
12	XII
15	XV
20	XX
30	XXX
40	XL
50	L
60	LX
70	LXX
80	LXXX
90	XC
100	C
200	CC
300	CCC
400	CD
500	D
600	DC
700	DCC
800	DCCC
900	CM
1000	M
1500	MD
2000	MM

Ephemera
Reference Numbers

There are many ways of dating an item of paper ephemera, from the material it is made out of, the way the date is formatted, the way it is printed, or even down to the type of ink scribbled on it.

Many items of ephemera can be identified from a reference number allocated on the printed matter.

For example:

A Home Office booklet could have a reference 407659 7/27

In this case, the last three digits give the clue to the publishing date:

July 1927.

Ephemera
Date Identifier

When a day of the week and the month is known and a specific year is only suspected, the charts on the following pages will help confirm the year. However, it must be stressed that this is merely a guide.

Instructions:

1. Use List 1 to link a letter (between A and N) to your chosen year.

2. Refer to List 2 and select the relevant letter from those running across the top.

3. Go to the known month and read off the number between 01 and 28.

4. Refer to List 3 and select the relevant number between 01 and 28, this will then give you the day of the week.

Example:

If you have a day and month (Monday 12th August) and suspect that the year is 1963, select column D in List 2, then go to box 14 in List 3. This confirms your suspicion because the 12th August 1963 was a Monday.

List 1

					1800-E	1801-A
1802-B	1803-C	1804-H	1805-D	1806-E	1807-A	1808-I
1809-F	1810-G	1811-D	1812-J	1813-B	1814-C	1815-F
1816-K	1817-E	1818-A	1819-B	1820-L	1821-G	1822-D
1823-E	1824-M	1825-C	1826-F	1827-G	1828-N	1829-A
1830-B	1831-C	1832-H	1833-D	1834-E	1835-A	1836-I
1837-F	1838-G	1839-D	1840-J	1841-B	1842-C	1843-F
1844-K	1845-E	1846-A	1847-B	1848-L	1849-G	1850-D
1851-E	1852-M	1853-C	1854-F	1855-G	1856-N	1857-A
1858-B	1859-C	1860-H	1861-D	1862-E	1863-A	1864-I
1865-F	1866-G	1867-D	1868-J	1869-B	1870-C	1871-F
1872-K	1873-E	1874-A	1875-B	1876-L	1877-G	1878-D
1879-E	1880-M	1881-C	1882-F	1883-G	1884-N	1885-A
1886-B	1887-C	1888-H	1889-D	1890-E	1891-A	1892-I
1893-F	1894-G	1895-D	1896-J	1897-B	1898-C	1899-F
1900-G	1901-D	1902-E	1903-A	1904-I	1905-F	1906-G
1907-D	1908-J	1909-B	1910-C	1911-F	1912-K	1913-E
1914-A	1915-B	1916-L	1917-G	1918-D	1919-E	1920-M
1921-C	1922-F	1923-G	1924-N	1925-A	1926-B	1927-C
1928-H	1929-D	1930-E	1931-A	1932-I	1933-F	1934-G
1935-D	1936-J	1937-B	1938-C	1939-F	1940-K	1941-E
1942-A	1943-B	1944-L	1945-G	1946-D	1947-E	1948-M
1949-C	1950-F	1951-G	1952-N	1953-A	1954-B	1955-C
1956-H	1957-D	1958-E	1959-A	1960-I	1961-F	1962-G
1963-D	1964-J	1965-B	1966-C	1967-F	1968-K	1969-E
1970-A	1971-B	1972-L	1973-G	1974-D	1975-E	1976-M
1977-C	1978-F	1979-G	1980-N	1981-A	1982-B	1983-C
1984-H	1985-D	1986-E	1987-A	1988-I	1989-F	1990-G
1991-D	1992-J	1993-B	1994-C	1995-F	1996-K	1997-E
1998-A	1999-B	2000-L	2001-G	2002-D	2003-E	2004-M
2005-C	2006-F					

List 2

	A	B	C	D	E	F	G	H	I	J	K	L	M	N
Jan.	14	20	19	16	15	18	17	18	20	15	17	19	14	16
Feb.	11	10	09	06	05	08	07	01	03	12	28	02	04	27
Mar.	18	17	16	20	19	15	14	14	16	18	20	15	17	19
Apr.	22	21	13	24	23	26	25	25	13	22	24	26	21	23
May	20	19	18	15	14	17	16	16	18	20	15	17	19	14
June	24	23	22	26	25	21	13	13	22	24	26	21	23	25
July	15	14	20	17	16	19	18	18	20	15	17	19	14	16
Aug.	19	18	17	14	20	16	15	15	17	19	14	16	18	20
Sep.	23	22	21	25	24	13	26	26	21	23	25	13	22	24
Oct.	14	20	19	16	15	18	17	17	19	14	16	18	20	15
Nov.	25	24	23	13	26	22	21	21	23	25	13	22	24	26
Dec.	16	15	14	18	17	20	19	19	14	16	18	20	15	17

List 3

1

Su	Mo	Tu	We	Th	Fr	Sa
			01	02	03	04
05	06	07	08	09	10	11
12	13	14	15	16	17	18
19	20	21	22	23	24	25
26	27	28	29			

2

Su	Mo	Tu	We	Th	Fr	Sa
		01	02	03	04	05
06	07	08	09	10	11	12
13	14	15	16	17	18	19
20	21	22	23	24	25	26
27	28	29				

3

Su	Mo	Tu	We	Th	Fr	Sa
	01	02	03	04	05	06
07	08	09	10	11	12	13
14	15	16	17	18	19	20
21	22	23	24	25	26	27
28	29					

4

Su	Mo	Tu	We	Th	Fr	Sa
01	02	03	04	05	06	07
08	09	10	11	12	13	14
15	16	17	18	19	20	21
22	23	24	25	26	27	28
29						

5

Su	Mo	Tu	We	Th	Fr	Sa
						01
02	03	04	05	06	07	08
09	10	11	12	13	14	15
16	17	18	19	20	21	22
23	24	25	26	27	28	

6

Su	Mo	Tu	We	Th	Fr	Sa
					01	02
03	04	05	06	07	08	09
10	11	12	13	14	15	16
17	18	19	20	21	22	23
24	25	26	27	28		

List 3 continued...

7

Su	Mo	Tu	We	Th	Fr	Sa
				01	02	03
04	05	06	07	08	09	10
11	12	13	14	15	16	17
18	19	20	21	22	23	24
25	26	27	28			

8

Su	Mo	Tu	We	Th	Fr	Sa
			01	02	03	04
05	06	07	08	09	10	11
12	13	14	15	16	17	18
19	20	21	22	23	24	25
26	27	28				

9

Su	Mo	Tu	We	Th	Fr	Sa
		01	02	03	04	05
06	07	08	09	10	11	12
13	14	15	16	17	18	19
20	21	22	23	24	25	26
27	28					

10

Su	Mo	Tu	We	Th	Fr	Sa
	01	02	03	04	05	06
07	08	09	10	11	12	13
14	15	16	17	18	19	20
21	22	23	24	25	26	27
28						

11

Su	Mo	Tu	We	Th	Fr	Sa
01	02	03	04	05	06	07
08	09	10	11	12	13	14
15	16	17	18	19	20	21
22	23	24	25	26	27	28

12

Su	Mo	Tu	We	Th	Fr	Sa
						01
02	03	04	05	06	07	08
09	10	11	12	13	14	15
16	17	18	19	20	21	22
23	24	25	26	27	28	29

List 3 continued...

13

Su	Mo	Tu	We	Th	Fr	Sa
					01	02
03	04	05	06	07	08	09
10	11	12	13	14	15	16
17	18	19	20	21	22	23
24	25	26	27	28	29	30

14

Su	Mo	Tu	We	Th	Fr	Sa
				01	02	03
04	05	06	07	08	09	10
11	12	13	14	15	16	17
18	19	20	21	22	23	24
25	26	27	28	29	30	31

15

Su	Mo	Tu	We	Th	Fr	Sa
			01	02	03	04
05	06	07	08	09	10	11
12	13	14	15	16	17	18
19	20	21	22	23	24	25
26	27	28	29	30	31	

16

Su	Mo	Tu	We	Th	Fr	Sa
		01	02	03	04	05
06	07	08	09	10	11	12
13	14	15	16	17	18	19
20	21	22	23	24	25	26
27	28	29	30	31		

17

Su	Mo	Tu	We	Th	Fr	Sa
	01	02	03	04	05	06
07	08	09	10	11	12	13
14	15	16	17	18	19	20
21	22	23	24	25	26	27
28	29	30	31			

18

Su	Mo	Tu	We	Th	Fr	Sa
01	02	03	04	05	06	07
08	09	10	11	12	13	14
15	16	17	18	19	20	21
22	23	24	25	26	27	28
29	30	31				

List 3 continued...

19

Su	Mo	Tu	We	Th	Fr	Sa
						01
02	03	04	05	06	07	08
09	10	11	12	13	14	15
16	17	18	19	20	21	22
23	24	25	26	27	28	29
30	31					

20

Su	Mo	Tu	We	Th	Fr	Sa
					01	02
03	04	05	06	07	08	09
10	11	12	13	14	15	16
17	18	19	20	21	22	23
24	25	26	27	28	29	30
31						

21

Su	Mo	Tu	We	Th	Fr	Sa
				01	02	03
04	05	06	07	08	09	10
11	12	13	14	15	16	17
18	19	20	21	22	23	24
25	26	27	28	29	30	

22

Su	Mo	Tu	We	Th	Fr	Sa
			01	02	03	04
05	06	07	08	09	10	11
12	13	14	15	16	17	18
19	20	21	22	23	24	25
26	27	28	29	30		

23

Su	Mo	Tu	We	Th	Fr	Sa
		01	02	03	04	05
06	07	08	09	10	11	12
13	14	15	16	17	18	19
20	21	22	23	24	25	26
27	28	29	30			

24

Su	Mo	Tu	We	Th	Fr	Sa
	01	02	03	04	05	06
07	08	09	10	11	12	13
14	15	16	17	18	19	20
21	22	23	24	25	26	27
28	29	30				

List 3 continued...

25

Su	Mo	Tu	We	Th	Fr	Sa
01	02	03	04	05	06	07
08	09	10	11	12	13	14
15	16	17	18	19	20	21
22	23	24	25	26	27	28
29	30					

26

Su	Mo	Tu	We	Th	Fr	Sa
						01
02	03	04	05	06	07	08
09	10	11	12	13	14	15
16	17	18	19	20	21	22
23	24	25	26	27	28	29
30						

27

Su	Mo	Tu	We	Th	Fr	Sa
					01	02
03	04	05	06	07	08	09
10	11	12	13	14	15	16
17	18	19	20	21	22	23
24	25	26	27	28	29	

28

Su	Mo	Tu	We	Th	Fr	Sa
				01	02	03
04	05	06	07	08	09	10
11	12	13	14	15	16	17
18	19	20	21	22	23	24
25	26	27	28	29		

Old Money

£ (or L)	= pound (quid).
s	= shilling (bob). One shilling = 1/-. 20/- = £1.
d	= pence.
6d	= Sixpence (tanner).
12d	= One pence (1/-).

Crown	= 5/-.
Half Crown	= 2/6d.
Florin	= 2/-.

Decimal equivalent	= 240d = £1= 100 new pence.
Ten shillings	= 50p.
2/-	= 10p.
1/-	= 5p.

COIN	OLD VALUE	CEASED CIRCULATION
Farthing	¼ d	1956
Half penny	½ d	1967
One penny	1d	1967
Three pence (silver)	3d	1944
Three pence	3d	1967
Groat	4d	1887
Six pence	6d	1967
One shilling	1/-	1967
Two shillings (Florin)	2/-	1967
Half Crown	2/6d	1967
Crown	5/-	Still minted today with £5 face value.
Ten shilling note	10/-	Last printed 1969
One pound note		1983

Hallmark Identification

British hallmarks (a guarantee of an item's purity or quality) include a purity mark, an assay office mark, a date (letter), and sometimes a maker's mark.

On gold:

The purity mark of a crown with the carat was used from 1798 to 1975, but in Scotland a thistle replaced the crown.

From 1798 to 1854 only gold assays at 18ct and 22ct were hallmarked, with 9ct, 12ct, and 15ct being introduced thereafter. The fineness (in thousandths) was added for the period 1854 to 1932.

After 1975, gold marks were standardised and the only marks used were the crown and the fineness in thousandths, along with the place of assay and the date (letter).

On silver:

The lion passant means sterling silver, but as with gold, a thistle was used on Scottish products until 1975. Some items made of a higher Britannia silver standard were marked with the figure of Britannia instead of the lion. All items produced between 1697 and 1720 carry the Britannia mark.

Hallmark Identification
(Assay Marks)

The origin of an item can be determined by its assay mark.

 London's leopard head. First used 1300.
The leopard was crowned during the period 1478 - 1822.

 Birmingham's anchor. First used 1773.
Usually marked sideways on gold and upright on silver.

 Chester's shield. First used 1701. Last used 1962.

 Dublin's harp. First used 1636.

 Edinburgh's castle. First used 1681. Last used 1974.

 Exeter's castle. First used 1701. Last used 1883.

 Glasgow's tree insignia. First used 1681. Last used 1964.

 Newcastle's three towers. First used 1702. Last used 1884.

 Sheffield's crown. First used 1773.

 York's pennant flag. First used 1560. Last used 1858.

Special note: Watch out for the special 'year 2000' cross hallmark introduced for some items to celebrate the Millennium.

Hallmark Identification
(Date Letters)

Each assay office has its own cycle of hallmarks, which include a letter for each year.

Year letter cycles start at A and usually end at Z. However, some cycles end before the letter Z is reached, and some cycles do not include the letter J.

In order to distinguish between years, in each cycle the letters are designed differently. For example, with a London hallmark the letter M signifying a date of 1807 is significantly different to the M used in the following cycle (which signifies a date of 1827).

There are hundreds of different date letters, too many to list in a book of this size, but thankfully there are plenty of good hallmark and date letter guides available in books and on the Internet.

British Patent Numbers

There was never a set rule on how to cite a British patent on an item.

Older items often have only the name of the inventor or the company. Some items have application numbers even if the patent wasn't granted.

British patents were not issued with numbers until October 1852. Numbers were then issued retrospectively to 1617, as well as forward from then on. It is not likely that an item made before 1852 will have a patent number.

The following tables should help you to identify the year of many British patent numbers.

British Patents
(1617 - 1852)

Until 1852 patents were acquired through a system that required visiting seven different offices and two signatures by the monarch.

Patents granted under this system were not numbered, but following the modernisation of the patent law in 1852, 14359 patents up to that date were given numbers retrospectively.

The following chart gives the earliest patent number issued for each of the years in the period.

All numbers in the table would be appended by a slash and the year of issue. For example, the earliest patent number issued for 1617 would be displayed as: 'no. 2/1617'.

YEAR	EARLIEST PATENT NO	YEAR	EARLIEST PATENT NO
1617	2	1780	1243
1630	49	1790	1720
1640	124	1800	2367
1660	128	1805	2807
1670	159	1810	3291
1680	210	1815	3871
1690	263	1820	4428
1700	365	1825	5064
1710	396	1830	5879
1720	425	1835	6743
1730	514	1840	8331
1740	570	1845	10453
1750	652	1850	12918
1760	744	1852	14359
1770	949		

British Patents
(1852 - 1915)

In this period, patent applications filed were numbered starting at 1 each year. Any patents granted would retain the same number.

This means that patent numbers were regularly repeated during this period.

The following chart gives the number of patent applications in each year. This number also indicates the highest possible patent number granted for each of those years.

YEAR	NUMBER OF APPLICATIONS	YEAR	NUMBER OF APPLICATIONS
1852 - 53	4256	1885	16101
1854	2764	1886	17174
1855	2958	1887	18051
1856	3106	1888	19103
1857	3200	1889	21008
1858	3007	1890	21307
1859	3000	1891	22878
1860	3196	1892	24179
1861	3276	1893	25107
1862	3490	1894	25386
1863	3309	1895	25062
1864	3260	1896	30193
1865	3386	1897	30958
1866	3453	1898	27650
1867	3723	1899	25800
1868	3991	1900	23924
1869	3786	1901	26788
1870	3405	1902	28972
1871	3529	1903	28854
1872	3970	1904	29702
1873	4294	1905	27577
1874	4492	1906	30030
1875	4561	1907	28915
1876	5069	1908	28598
1877	4949	1909	30603
1878	5343	1910	30388
1879	5338	1911	29353
1880	5517	1912	30089
1881	5751	1913	30077
1882	6241	1914	24820
1883	5993	1915	18191
1884	17110		

British Patents
(1916 - 1981)

Since 1916 published patents have been numbered in a series starting at 100,001.

After 1916 it is generally the case that only granted patents were published, and there is no information available for those that were not granted.

Numbers are preceded by the letters 'GB' to denote a Great British patent number.

The following table shows the earliest patent number published for each year from 1916 up to and including 1981.

YEAR	EARLIEST PATENT NO	YEAR	EARLIEST PATENT NO
1916	100,001	1949	614,704
1917	102,812	1950	633,754
1918	112,131	1951	650,021
1919	121,611	1952	667,061
1920	136,852	1953	687,841
1921	155,801	1954	704,741
1922	173,241	1955	724,991
1923	190,732	1956	745,421
1924	208,751	1957	768,941
1925	226,571	1958	791,071
1926	244,801	1959	809,321
1927	263,501	1960	829,181
1928	282,701	1961	861,801
1929	302,941	1962	889,571
1930	323,171	1963	918,311
1931	340,201	1964	949,031
1932	363,615	1965	982,551
1933	385,258	1966	1,015,491
1934	407,311	1967	1,058,501
1935	421,246	1968	1,102,801
1936	439,856	1969	1,142,501
1937	458,491	1970	1,180,651
1938	477,016	1971	1,222,451
1939	497,409	1972	1,263,601
1940	512,178	1973	1,306,401
1941	530,617	1974	1,346,401
1942	542,024	1975	1,384,031
1943	550,067	1976	1,424,101
1944	558,091	1977	1,464,401
1945	566,191	1978	1,500,801
1946	574,006	1979	1,540,351
1947	583,360	1980	1,560,781
1948	595,746	1981	1,584,611

British Patents
(1979 - Present)

The Patent Act of 1977 started January 1, 1978. Patent applications filed under the act are published 18 months after their priority date (so the first patents under the act were published 1979).

The numbers under the Patent Act start at 2,000,001. Patents filed before the introduction of the Patent Act, but published after, still used the old numbering system (see previous table).

The letters 'GB' before the number denote that it is a Great British patent number.

YEAR	EARLIEST PATENT NO
1979	2,000,001
1980	2,023,381
1981	2,050,131
1982	2,078,071
1983	2,100,561
1984	2,121,661
1985	2,141,611
1986	2,160,751
1987	2,176,681
1988	2,192,121
1989	2,206,271
1990	2,220,118
1991	2,232,862
1992	2,245,131
1993	2,257,003
1994	2,268,036
1995	2,279,218
1996	2,290,445
1997	2,302,005
1998	2,314,495
1999	2,326,809
2000	2,338,877
2001	2,351,428
2002	2,363,560
2003	2,377,151
2004	2,390,285
2005	2,403,389
2006	2,415,592
2007	2,427,532
2008	2,439,518

The Reign Of British Monarchs From 1714

GEORGE I	1714 - 1727
GEORGE II	1727 - 1760
GEORGE III	1760 - 1820
GEORGE IV	1820 - 1830
WILLIAM IV	1830 - 1837
VICTORIA	1837 - 1901
EDWARD VII	1901 - 1910
GEORGE V	1910 - 1936
EDWARD VIII	1936 - 1936
GEORGE VI	1936 - 1952
ELIZABETH II	1952 - present

Items bearing the Tudor Crown (arched top) will date from 1902 to 1952.

Anything made after 1952 will bear the St Edwards Crown (which has an arch on either side of the top cross).

Doctor Who

Doctor Who appeared on the BBC November 23, 1963. It was suspended as an ongoing series in 1989 by the Controller of BBC One, Jonathan Powell.

The show went back into production in 2004, with the new series debut airing March 26, 2005.

The Doctors:

1963 - 66	William Hartnell
1966 - 69	Patrick Troughton
1970 - 74	Jon Pertwee
1974 - 81	Tom Baker
1981 - 84	Peter Davison
1984 - 86	Colin Baker
1987 - 89 + 1996	Sylvester McCoy
1996	Paul McGann
2005	Chris Eccleston
2005 - Present	David Tennant
Due to take over in 2010	Matt Smith

Note: Many others actors have portrayed the Doctor in novels, radio shows, stage productions and television specials.

AA Badge Number
Identification

The numbers on AA badges were issue numbers. They give a good indication of when a badge was produced:

- 1 to 999,999 - 1906-30
- A-P suffixes - 1930-45
- RST suffixes - 1946-56
(Flat motorcycle badges)
- WXYZA suffixes - 1956-67
(Domed motorcycle badges)
- OA to OZ prefixes - 1945-57
- 1A-9A prefix - 1957-59
- 1B-9B prefix - 1960-61
- 1C-9C prefix - 1962-63
- 1D-9D prefix - 1964-65
- 1E-9E prefix - 1966-67

**AA Grille Badge.
Sold 20 Feb 2006
for £20.00**

After 1967, the badge became square and there was no longer any number on it.

**AA Square Grille Badge.
Sold 22 June 2005
for £10.00**

Acronyms

AA	American Airlines.
AA	Automobile Association.
ACF	Automobile Club de France.
AD	Anno Domini.
AFS	Auxiliary Fire Service.
AMC	Army Medical Corps.
ARP	Air Raid Precautions.
ASA	Advertising Standards Authority.
ASC	Army Service Corps.
AT&T	American Telephone and Telegraph.
BA	British Airways (formerly BEA).
BBC	British Broadcasting Corporation.
BBFC	British Board of Film Classification.
BC	Before Christ.
BC	British Columbia.
BEA	British European Airways.
BEF	British Expeditionary Forces.
BM	British Midland (airline).
BMA	British Medical Association.
BMC	British Motor Corporation.
BMW	Bayerische Motoren Werke.
BO	British Officer.
BOAC	British Overseas Airway Corporation.
BP	Blue Peter.
BP	British Petroleum.
BR	British Rail.
BSA	Birmingham Small Arms.
BSI	British Standards Institution.
BT	British Telecommunications.
DC	Detective Comics.
DJ	Dust Jacket (of a book).
DVD	Digital Versatile Disc.

EP	Extended Play (record).
EU	European Union.
GMC	General Medical Council.
GMC	General Motors Corporation.
HA	Health Authority.
HM	Her (or His) Majesty.
HMS	Her (or His) Majesty's Ship.
HRH	Her (or His) Royal Highness.
ISBN	International Standard Book Number.
ISO	International Standards Organisation.
ITV	International Television.
KLM	Royal Dutch Airline.
LP	Long Playing (record).
MBE	Member of the Order of the British Empire.
MC	Military Cross.
MGM	Metro Goldwyn Mayer.
MP	Member of Parliament
MP	Military Police.
MS	Manuscript.
MS	Microsoft.
MS	Motor Ship.
NATO	North Atlantic Treaty Organisation.
NCO	Non-Commissioned Officer.
NHS	National Health Service.
NSC	National Screening Committee.
NTWF	National Transport Workers' Federation.
OBE	Officer of the Order of the British Empire.
PO	Petty Officer.
PO	Post Office.
P&O	Pacific and Orient.
RA	Royal Academy.
RA	Royal Artillery.
RAC	Royal Armoured Corps.
RAC	Royal Automobile Club.

RAF	Royal Air Force.
RAOC	Royal Army Ordnance Corps.
RASC	Royal Army Service Corps (ASC prior to 1918).
RCT	Royal Corps of Transport.
RE	Royal Engineers.
REME	Royal Electrical and Mechanical Engineers.
RM	Royal Mail.
RMS	Royal Mail Ship.
RMS	Royal Merchant Ship.
RoSPA	Royal Society for the Prevention of Accidents.
RPM	Revolutions Per Minute.
RR	Rolls-Royce.
RSPB	Royal Society for the Protection of Birds.
RSPCA	Royal Society for the Prevention of Cruelty to Animals.
RSPCC	Royal Society for the Prevention of Cruelty to Children.
SNCF	Societe Nationale des Chemins de fer Francais.
SS	Steam Ship.
TA	Territorial Army.
TGWU	Transport and General Workers Union.
TRH	Their Royal Highnesses.
TWA	Trans World Airlines.
UN	United Nations.
USAF	United States Air Force.
USS	United States Ship.
VAT	Value Added Tax.
VHS	Video Home System.
WCW	World Championship Wrestling.
WO	Warrant Officer.
WWE	World Wrestling Entertainment.
WWF	World Wildlife Fund.
WWW	World Wide Web.

Subject Terminology and Glossary

ACETATE - A record pressing made of aluminium with a coating of vinyl-like material, used for checking the quality of work in progress being recorded by a producer and artist. They are only designed for a few plays as the coating quickly wears out.

ADDORSED - Back to back.

AERONAUTICA - Collectable items relating to aircraft.

AEROPHILATELY - The collecting of air mail stamps and covers.

ALLOY - A mixture of metals.

AMERICANA - Items that are distinctive of America.

ANTHOLOGY - Collection of literary passages and works.

ARABESQUE - Symmetrical decoration in the form of flowing lines of branches, leaves and scrolling.

ARCTOPHILY - The collecting of teddy bears.

ARGYROTHECOLOGY - The collection and study of money boxes.

ART DÉCO - A style of interior decoration and manufactured objects, of the period (approximately) 1925 – 1940. Symmetrical designs adapted to mass production.

ART NOUVEAU - A style of decoration of the early 20th century. Based on soft curves and influenced by the example of Japanese art (particularly leaves and flowers).

ARTEFACT - An object shaped by human craft (such as a tool), usually with archaeological significance.

ASTROPHILATELY - Space related postage stamps.

AUDIOPHILY - The collecting of recorded sound.

AURICULAR - Shaped like the ear.

AUTOMOBILIA - Items relating to motor vehicles.

BACK STAMP - A maker's marking on the underside of a ceramic piece. (Back Stamps scored through, indicate 'seconds').

BANDOPHILY - The collecting of cigar bands.

BEZEL - The metal frame around the glass of a watch or clock.

BIBLIOLOGY - The study of books.

BIBLIOPHILY - The collecting of books.

BIBLIOTICS - The study of documents to determine their authenticity.

BOOTERS - Buyers at a car boot sale.

BOXWOOD - Close grained light yellow wood of the box. A mustard spoon could typically be made of boxwood.

BREWERIANA - Collectable items related to brewing.

BUFFED - Condition description for a vinyl record, where the surface looks as though it has been buffed with wire wool. In other words, the surface is multi scratched in poor condition.

CAGOPHILY - The collecting of keys.

CAMEO - A shell or stone carved in relief, in such a way that brings out the different colours of the material used.

CARD CASE - A case (usually with an ornate design) to carry calling/business cards. Originated in 18th century France.

CARTOGRAPHY - The study, making, and collecting of maps.

CARTOPHILY - The collecting of cigarette cards.

CAST IRON - Ironwork produced by pouring molten iron into a pre-shaped mould.

CERAMICS - The generic term for pottery, porcelain, terracotta, etc.

CHINOISERIE - Decorative artwork with Chinese characteristics.

CHIROGRAPHY - The study of handwriting.

CHRYSOLOGY - The study of precious metals.

CHURCHILLANIA - Collectable items relating to Winston Churchill.

CLYVESOPHILY - Collecting of mugs.

CODICOLOGY - The study of early manuscripts.

CONCHOLOGY - The study of shells.

COPOCLEPHILY - The collecting of key rings.

COTTAPENSOPHILY - Collecting of coat hangers.

CRAZING - A fine network of cracks in the glaze of pottery and porcelain.

CRIMINOLOGY - The study of criminals and crime.

CRYPTOLOGY - The study of codes.

DACTYLIOLOGY - The study of rings.

DECAL - Short for decalcomania. The art or process of transferring a design from prepared paper onto another surface.

DELFTWARE - Earthenware named after the Dutch town of Delft.

DELTIOLOGY - The collecting of postcards.

DIECAST - Zinc alloy used to manufacture toys, enabling the production of strong, shiny, bright, permanently decorated items.

DIGITABULIST - The collecting of thimbles.

DISCOPHILY - The collecting of recorded music.

DISNEYANA - Collectable items relating to Disney.

EARTHENWARE - Glazed pottery fired to a temperature of approximately 1000 degrees C. Normally red or brown with a low chipping resistance.

ECCLESIOLOGY - The study and collection of items relating to church.

EDWARDIAN - Relating to the period of the reign of King Edward VII (1901 – 1910).

EGYPTOLOGY - The study of Ancient Egypt.

ENAMEL - A semi-opaque form of glass fused on to metal surfaces to decorate them.

ENCRUST - To ornament by overlaying with a crust of something precious.

ENIGMATOLOGY - The study and collecting of puzzles.

EPHEMERA - Anything designed to be used and then thrown away, usually made of paper. For example, old bus tickets and cigarette packets.

EPNS - Electro Plated Silver Nickel - silver plate.

EROTICA - Glamour related items.

ESCAPEMENT - Mechanical device that regulates the movement in a watch or clock.

ESCUTCHEON - Protective plate around a key hole, etc. Also in nautical terms – a ship's nameplate affixed to the stern.

ETYMOLOGY - The study of the origin of words.

EXONUMIA - The US word for coin-like objects (and the collecting of them).

FLATWARE- Tableware that is relatively flat and fashioned as a single unit (e.g. the meal-tray supplied by airlines). Also flat cutlery.

FLIPBACK - Vinyl record (picture) sleeve, laminated on the front only, with short fold-overs on the reverse. Most common in the sixties.

FOXING - Discolouration of paper, wood, etc., with spots through ageing and mildew.

FRESCO - The art of painting in water-colour on plaster or mortar when not quite dry.

FROMOLOGY - Cheese label collecting.

FUSILATELY - The collecting of phone cards.

GEMMOLOGY - The study of jewels and gems.

GEORGIAN - Relating to the period of the four King Georges, 1714 – 1830.

GILDED - Covered with a thin layer of gold.

GLYPTOGRAPHY - The art of engraving on gemstones.

GLYPTOLOGY - The study of gem engravings.

GNOMONICS - Items relating to the measuring of time with sundials.

GUTTER - The selvedge (borders) of a sheet of postage stamps, either unprinted or with plate numbers or other markings.

HALLMARK - A mark punched on to articles to guarantee a statutory degree of purity. Four stamps are; maker's mark, mark of quality, mark of the hall of Assay, and the year mark.

HISTORIOGRAPHY - The study of writing history.

HISTORIOLOGY - Study of history.

HOPLOLOGY - The study of weaponry.

HOROGRAPHY - The art of constructing sundials or clocks.

HOROLOGY - The science of time measurement.

HOSTELAPHILY - The collecting of outdoor signs from inns.

HYMNOGRAPHY - The study of writing hymns.

HYMNOLOGY - The study of hymns.

ICONOLOGY - The study of icons and symbols.

INFUNABULIST - See 'Bandophily'.

JUVENALIA - Children's play items.

KITCHENALIA - Items relating to a kitchen.

KITSCH - Arguably, a tacky version of 'retro'. Popular because of its garishness and links to a particular era (largely 50s/60s/70s).

LABEORPHILY - The collecting of beer bottle labels.

LACLABPHILY - See 'Fromology'.

LACQUER - The application of several layers of paint and special varnish to produce a decorative surface.

LAPIDARY - Cutting and engraving precious stones.

LEPIDOPTEROLOGY - The study of butterflies and moths.

LITHOGRAPHY - A process of printing dating back to the end of the eighteenth century (discovered in Germany). The principle being that oil and water do not mix. The image is drawn with a special applicator on a flat surface over which water is then passed. When covered with ink, only the applied area will accept it.

LOTOLOGY - The collecting of scratch cards and lottery related items.

LUCITE - Transparent thermoplastic acrylic resin.

LUSTRE - A glaze - surface coating for ceramics creating shine.

MAGIRICS - The art of cookery.

MATT GLAZE - A dull-surfaced glaze, non-reflecting.

MEMORABILIA - Items to commemorate memorable events.

MILITARIA - Collecting of materials or objects relating to the military.

MISCELLANY - A whole variety of objects. Miscellaneous items.

MODERNIST - A style characteristic of modern times.

MYTHOLOGY - The study of myths and fables.

NETSUKE - Traditional Japanese clothing, such as the kimono, had no pockets, so it was necessary for people to carry items like pipes and tobacco in containers called sagemono. These sagemono were hung from the sash of the kimono (the obi), and were secured in place using specially carved toggles known as netsuke.

NOTAPHILY - The collecting of bank notes.

NUMISMATICS - The collecting of and study of coins.

OBJECTS OF VIRTU - Fine art objects and antiques.

OBJETS D'ART - As 'objects of virtu'.

OBVERSE - The side of a coin, or medal, on which the head or principal design is shown. The other side of the coin is called the 'reverse'.

OENOLOGY - The study of wine.

OLEOGRAPH - A lithographic reproduction of an oil painting.

OOLOGY - The collecting of and study of bird's eggs.

OPERCULISM - Collecting of milk tops.

PALAEOBIOLOGY - The study of fossil plants and animals.

PALEONTOLOGY - The study of ancient life and fossils.

PAPIER-MACHE - Layers of paper shredded into a pulp and then pressed into shapes.

PAPYROLOGY - The study of paper.

PARANUMISTMATICA - The UK word for coin-like objects (and the collecting of them). A sub-category of 'Numismatics'.

PARAPHERNALIA - Miscellany associated with particular interests and items.

PARURE - A full matching jewellery set comprising necklace, brooch, bracelet, and earrings.

PETROLIANA - Gas and oil related items.

PHILATELY - Stamp collecting and the study of postal history.

PHILLUMENY - The collecting of matchboxes and matchbox labels.

PHILOGRAPHY - Autograph collecting.

PHILOMETRY - Collecting of First Day Covers.

PHONOPHILY - See 'Discophily'.

PICTURE DISC - A record pressed on clear vinyl, the middle of which is sandwiched with a picture. These are sometimes in shapes other than circular.

PORCELAIN - White form of stoneware usually translucent. Hard and non-porous. The most highly refined of all clay bodies and requiring the highest firing.

PRODUCTION STILLS - Are photographs taken during the production of a motion picture. They are usually shot during principal photography, and show the interaction between the actors and director, camera crew, makeup and wardrobe department, or stunt team.

PROOF - Early impression of a stamp, coin or medal, struck as a specimen.

PROVENANCE - Proof of past ownership or of authenticity.

RAILWAYANA - Collectable items relating to the railway.

REGENCY - The style of furniture, buildings, literature etc., popular in Great Britain 1811 – 1820.

RETRO - A fashion design, décor or style reminiscent of things past.

RETRO CHIC - Stylish and elegant retro.

RETROPHILIA - A love for things of the past.

REVERSE - Of a coin or medal (see 'Obverse').

RHYKENOLOGY - The collection and study of woodworking tools.

ROCOCO - Typically European architectural and decorative asymmetrical designs of the first half of the eighteenth century.

RPM - (Revolutions per minute), the speed at which a record is designed to play.

SCRIPOPHILY - The collecting of old financial documents, such as stocks and bonds certificates.

SEPIA - A brown ink or pigment. A photograph in a brown tint.

SHAGREEN - The rough hide of a shark or ray. Untanned leather with a granular surface that is often dyed green.

SIDEROGRAPHY - The art of engraving on steel.

SOCIOLOGY - The study of society.

SOLANDER BOX - A box designed to hold manuscripts, maps, books, etc. Named after Dr. Daniel Solander (1736 – 1782).

SPELTER - Zinc based metal, often called 'poor man's bronze'. Normally thinner and tinnier than bronze but of similar appearance.

STANHOPE - Novelty item with a tiny lens that reveals a photograph when held to light.

STIPPLE - Decoration consisting of tiny dots in an overall pattern.

STONEWARE - Glazed pottery in which both body and glaze are fused together.

SUCROLOGY - The collecting of sugar packets.

TAT - Tasteless, not worthy of serious collecting (by most people), tatty and generally of little value.

TAXIDERMY - The art of stuffing and mounting the skins of animals to give life-like appearances.

TEEKIN - American term for 'antiquing' (buying, browsing, selling).

TEGESTOLOGY - The collecting of beer mats.

TEST PRESSING - The first factory pressings of the record. For circulation to reviewers. Often plain white labels.

TOBACCIANA - Smoking related collectable items.

TREEN - Small wooden objects. Not of joined construction, therefore furniture items not included.

TUNBRIDGEWARE - Decoratively inlaid woodwork, characteristic of Tunbridge, Kent 18th and 19th century. Often fashioned as a mosaic of varying coloured woods.

TURNERY - The art of turning in a lathe.

TYPOGRAPHY - The art of printing or using type.

UK QUADS - Film posters. Generally unique to the UK because they are landscape instead of portrait.

VECTURIST - Transport token collector.

VELOLOGY - The collecting of Vehicle Excise Licences (tax discs).

VENEER - A thin layer of wood used to surface or decorate a piece of furniture.

VEXILLOLOGY - The study of and collecting of flags and bunting.

VICTORIANA - Objects of the period of Queen Victoria's reign (1837 – 1901).

VITREOUS - Glass-like. Usually refers to a porcelain or stoneware fired body.

VITRICS - Glassware and the study of.

XYLOGRAPHY - The art of engraving on wood.

XYLOLOGY - The study of wood.

NOTES

TRADE AND COLLECT